Get the "F" Out!

Liberating FEAR & Letting LOVE In

CAROLYN BENNETT-SULLIVAN

Let your light shine.
All the best,
Carolyn Bennett Sullivan

ACKNOWLEDGMENTS

The idea for this book tapped me on the shoulder for a couple of years before I completed it. Without the support of others it could still just be an idea of something I'll do someday.

First I want to acknowledge all the teachers in my life which will remain unnamed. Those who have provided me with the opportunities for greater wisdom and growth through life's lessons and challenges; you are the ones who have helped me the most.

Now for those I will name. Jane Fenicle, my high school English teacher who encouraged me and built my confidence as a writer. Anna Marie Trotman, it was in your course that I was inspired to write this book. Tom Sterner, an author I respect and am fortunate to count as a friend and trusted advisor, your suggestions, wisdom, humor and guidance have been immeasurable.

To Ara-Atkinson-Skinner, illustrator and advisor extraordinaire, you helped make this book come alive. To Charlie McDermott for the kick in the ass to get it completed. And to Apryl Parcher, my editor, whose patience, knowledge and friendship guided me through uncharted waters. Thank you all.

Dedication

This book is dedicated to my parents, Audrey and Jim Bennett. Two of the most loving people on the planet, you have shown me the meaning of unconditional love through your actions, words and deeds. Thank you.

And to my daughter Cassidy, you are a bright shining light in my life. I love you to the Moon and back.

CONTENTS

INTRODUCTION

This book is about my journey to free myself from fear-based thinking and the process of re-connecting to the Divine power that's within me and within all of us. Many of us believe in a power greater than ourselves. Some call it God, Spirit, Source, Allah, Jehovah or Intuition. It has many names. It's the power of love, the Divine light and Intelligence that's within everyone. It guides us to greater fulfillment, peace and joy when we open ourselves to listening to its voice within us. It also gives us the strength, courage and power to step into the unknown, to follow a greater calling within ourselves when we trust it. It's the inner knowing of our true selves, that part of us that just knows "this is right." Remember a time when you followed your gut even if it didn't make sense and then marveled at the outcome of your decision?

Some of us feel a connection to this Divine Intelligence, others don't believe it exists. Most of us feel this connection at times and then are driven by our fear in our day to day lives. We're prodded and driven to think rationally and logically in our society. Our rational mind is often driven by our ego which tells us it doesn't make sense to follow your dreams, or you're not talented, experienced or have enough resources to pursue your passions. You may believe you're not one of those people. I used to think that too until I realized how it kept me stuck in patterns of self- sabotage.

Fear which is driven by our ego is insidious in its control of our minds and thinking. It seeps in where we don't expect it and causes us to shrink away from our inherent connection, beauty and love. It causes us to doubt our ability to live the life we desire, to experience the love and connection for which we long.

Deepak Chopra states: "The ego is our self-image, not our true self. It is characterized by labels, masks, images and judgments. The true self is the field of possibilities, creativity, intentions and power. We can go beyond the ego through self-awareness – awareness of our thoughts, feelings, behaviors and speech. Thus we begin to move slowly beyond the ego to the true self."

Author Wayne Dyer writes:

> "The ego-idea has been with us ever since we began to think. It sends us false messages about our true nature. It leads us to make assumptions about what will make us happy and we end up frustrated. It pushes us to promote our self-importance while we yearn for a deeper and richer life experience. It causes us to fall into the void of self-absorption again and again, not knowing that we need only shed the false idea of who we are.
>
> Our true self is eternal. It is the God force within us. The way of our higher self is to reflect our inner reality rather than the outer illusion."

He goes on to say the ego is "edging God out," and when we live from ego-based thinking, we're living from fear.

Marianne Williamson, author of *A Return to Love*, has said there are really only two emotions, love and fear. To recognize the ego's power over us is the first step to greater awareness of how fear-based thinking often controls our lives. From that awareness we can become conscious of choosing to act from fear or love. It's not an easy journey, for we are human after all. So as we navigate the peaks and valleys of our lives, we stumble and fall then make big leaps forward, learning how to liberate ourselves from fear's grip and to reconnect to the Divine power, the love that's within us.

It's a choice we make on a daily basis. Do we fall victim to the fear-based messages that bombard us continually or do we take a stand and step towards liberation? More and more people are beginning to make the call for love and cooperation and to create a world that works for everyone. Yes, times they are a changing. We have come to a pivotal moment here on Earth, an awakening from the chaos of the economic downturn, political upheaval and distrust in governments and corporations.. We are beginning to remember who we are. No longer do we desire to be merely cogs in the wheel for those who want to dominate our lives. The time has come for us to re-connect with our true selves. We want to embrace the power within ourselves, to know and trust the Divine spark that lives within every one of us—and the momentum is growing. We are awakening from the myth we've been told, from the lies that society has taught us, yet we find it difficult to let go and trust. Fear keeps us stuck even when we choose to move forward. I know because I've been there. I understand the calling to change your life, to embrace a better way of living. I also understand the hesitation (the obstacles) that fear produces through our egos to keep us stuck.

My mission is to help you recognize where it's got its grip on you and the not-so-obvious ways that fear manifests in your mindset, and to give you tools to help you liberate your mind from its control. Instead of allowing fear to control you, I want you to allow fear to be your teacher and honor the lessons you've learned because of it. You *can* become master over it—in fact, it's essential in order for you to get the F(ear) out and let love in. The time has come for us to re-connect with our true selves, to embrace the power within, to know and trust the Divine spark that lives within every one of us and to live our lives based on possibility, purpose and passion. It's time to liberate ourselves from living in fear to loving our lives. Just think of the difference we could make in our relationships, communities and the world by loving ourselves and our lives and living with a sense of purpose, joy and passion!

"WHAT IS NEEDED, RATHER THAN RUNNING AWAY OR CONTROLLING OR SUPPRESSING OR ANY OTHER RESISTANCE, IS UNDERSTANDING FEAR; THAT MEANS, WATCH IT, LEARN ABOUT IT COME DIRECTLY INTO CONTACT WITH IT. WE ARE TO LEARN ABOUT FEAR, NOT HOW TO ESCAPE FROM IT."

– JIDDU KRISHNAMURTI

"FEAR IS LIKE AN ANNOYING RELATIVE, YOU CAN TRY TO IGNORE IT OR YOU CAN LEARN TO LOVE IT FOR WHAT IT TEACHES YOU ABOUT YOURSELF."

- CAROLYN BENNETT-SULLIVAN

Chapter 1

Fear Is a Four Letter Word

I know fear very intimately; it's driven most of my life's decisions. I didn't grow up in poverty or experience years of abuse or neglect. I grew up in a middle class family, with parents who loved me and did the best they could to provide for their family. Why is it I've made the majority of my life decisions based on fear, fear of not being good enough, or trying to prove my worth? Like many people, I've been a people-pleaser the majority of my life basing my self-worth on what others thought of me and being nice. I'm an optimistic person naturally, and typically find the good in people and situations. Yet I've always had a timidity that has made asking for help a real challenge.

I spent New Year's Eve 2010 alone for the first time in fifteen years. My marriage that had been sinking deeper and deeper into emotional and financial debt finally collapsed during the summer of 2009. By the fall of 2009 we had separated.

In December we sold our house and I moved on the 30th. It was snowy and cold, and we were about to have one of the worst winters on record. I don't recommend moving in December if you live in the Northern hemisphere. It's not fun. So there I was unpacking boxes in the kitchen of an unfamiliar home that I just rented. My daughter was with her dad, and I was alone and scared. I have to admit there was a part of me that felt relieved to finally be divorcing. The weight of the stress of our marriage had taken its toll on me and on my ex-husband. I believe we were both worn out. The optimist in me believed that from here on out everything was going to turn around, that my life would once again be filled with wonderful new beginnings and adventures. I had bought a bottle of champagne to bring in the New Year and decided to treat myself to a bubble bath and a toast later in the evening after I got some unpacking completed. I remember sinking into the bubbly warm water, it was almost midnight, and toasting to a new beginning. Removing my engagement and wedding ring, my hand felt bare. I was filled with a mixture of emotions; sadness, relief, worry, and even a bit of excitement of what might lie ahead. Mostly I felt like a failure. I felt I had failed myself, my husband and our daughter by not being successful, and that I was a failure as a wife not living up to my husband's expectations (or my own).

During the last six years of my marriage I was a distributor in a direct sales business; and, despite my efforts, I hadn't made much money with it and had racked up credit card debt. I kept thinking my business was going to take off and be successful, and yet now I know it was fear-based beliefs that held me back. This was a constant source of stress in my marriage compounded by my husband's own fear-based thinking. It was a recipe for disaster over time as we sank deeper and deeper into a hole of financial duress, distrust and blame.

Divorce is the death of a marriage. One of the things we grieve the most during divorce is the loss of the dream. The dream of the vision you had when you got married, the dream of what could have been if only things had been different. For years I kept telling myself, if only I had done this better or changed that, our marriage would have been better. The fact is I felt miserable for many years of the marriage. Even without financial challenges, I believe it would have imploded. Fear kept me in my marriage. The fear of loss, of how I would support myself, the fear of failure, the fear of how the divorce would affect our daughter and the fear of what people would think. Fear is a powerful motivator.

It can be used to move us forward, but it typically holds us back and keeps us stuck.

One of the most popular acronyms for fear comes from Zig Zigler: "False Evidence Appearing Real." Although fear is false evidence (driven by a memory, belief or worry of the future), I believe it's more about resisting what is—resisting the now.

There are times when that false evidence feels very real. For example, if you have a bill that's due and there's not enough money in your bank account to pay for it, that feels very real. When you lose your job, get diagnosed with cancer, have a friend die, get divorced, or just have a bad day, it feels very real. We're constantly given the opportunity to choose between love and fear.

For me, F.E.A.R. is *Feelings Experienced as Resistance*. We all experience it; yet it's so pervasive in our culture and in our lives that we deny how much we're controlled and driven by it. How often do we stop ourselves from doing something that benefits us and moves us towards our dreams because of it? Fear is driven by our ego. And when the ego is controlling us, we're not connected to our true selves. We're not connected to the love from which we came.

During and after my divorce, I felt a lot of fear around money or the lack thereof. Although I was working a part-time job and had gone back to commission-only medical sales, I wasn't making enough to survive. My decision to re-enter medical sales was based on fear. It's what I knew even though I didn't enjoy it. In fact, I'd left the pharmaceutical industry seven years prior because I felt out of integrity with the entire Western medical system.

For the next year and a half, everything I tried failed. The companies I represented were mostly start-ups, and two of them disbanded their sales forces just as I was starting to earn money. Could I have gone out and gotten a job? Probably, yet I felt no one would want to hire me because I had not worked a full-time position in seven years and was over 50. Again my ego wrapped its fearful thoughts around my mind, and I sank deeper into depression. My self-esteem reached an all-time low. There were times I felt so dark that if it hadn't been for my daughter, I believe I would've seriously considered suicide.

I didn't really want to die, I just wanted the pain to stop. I wanted someone to rescue me from the hell I'd created in my mind. The fear (the resistance) came from my belief that I wasn't good enough, that I'd never have enough money, and the confusion of not knowing what to do or how to change things. Instead of focusing on a solution, I was focusing on my fear, on what I didn't want, and it became a self-fulfilling prophecy.

This is where the ego entangles us into believing that our worth is based on what we have, what we do, how much we make and how we look. It's so pervasive in our culture that we don't even realize its grip.

For instance, our news is filled with death, destruction, war, a poor economy... everything to make us fear the future and resist the good that's in our lives. Publications, games and TV shows are all fear-based. We have to live up to a particular standard or we're not good enough! Look at the violence on TV, in games and in movies. It's all about fear that something evil will destroy us; that we're victims and that without a hero we'll never survive.

What if we became our own hero's? What if we embraced the idea that the only way we can be a victim is if we *choose to be one?*

Putting Ego in its Place

So why do so many of us struggle with fear-based thinking? Why do we let it dominate us? The answer lies in our subconscious. In the introduction, I touched on the relationship we have with Divine love and ego, but let's take it a little further.

In *The Power of Now*, Eckard Tolle writes, "...ultimately all fear is the ego's fear of death, of annihilation. To the ego, death is always just around the corner. In this mind-identified state, fear of death affects every aspect of your life."

Gerald Jampolsky, M.D., psychiatrist and author of Love is Letting Go of Fear, states:

"The ego can be defined as our body/personality or lower self. It is the part of our mind that is split off or separated from our spiritual mind, which contains only God's loving thoughts. This split in our mind can be thought of as illusory; it can be contrasted to our true mind, a mind filled with love that is indivisible.

The thought system of the ego is based on guilt and fear. Its motto is, 'Seek but never find what you are looking for.' It is preoccupied with condemning judgments, attack and defense thoughts and is a master of deception. Its goal is to control everything and to believe it is right all the time. It expends an enormous amount of energy trying to predict the future based on our past experiences. The ego's world is a pleasure/pain world, and, for most of us, there is more pain than pleasure. It believes that if you don't fear the past and worry about the future, the world will fall apart. Separation is its game; so thinking of yourself first, getting and holding on to what little you can claim as your own, jealousy, possessiveness, and rejection are the core of its existence."

Our identity as defined by the ego is limited to the five senses; hearing, seeing, touching, smelling, and tasting. It is based on the interpretation and evaluation of what these senses feed back to our brain. It is a limited identity based on experiences of the past extending into the present and projected into the future. Seen through the eyes of the ego, my identity is my self-concept at any particular point in time, and is dependent on the opinions and judgments other people have about me, as well as the opinions and judgments I have about myself."

Based on these descriptions is it clearer how the ego derails us? Our ego is afraid of losing control over our thoughts. It does all that it can to keep us out of the present moment and disconnected from the Divine within, because when we choose to live from a place of connection and love, it annihilates our ego. Love is the death of the ego, and our ego will do anything to keep us from knowing real love. The ego wants us to fear death because once we embrace our connection to our true self, once we understand that we are eternal, the ego serves no purpose. It will do anything to keep us attached and dependent on its power over our thinking.

As humans, is there a place for our ego? Can we ever truly separate ourselves from it? It's part of our mind and yet we can learn to observe it, understand how it uses fear to control our minds and release its power over us. As long as we stay resistant to what is and stay separate from the present moment, our ego will dominate our mind through fear.

How do we change it? How do we learn to live our lives from a place of connection to ourselves, others and the Divine that lives within us? First by becoming aware of how fear is controlled by ego dominated thoughts and beliefs. Once it becomes a part of our awareness, it gives us the power to choose whether to allow the ego's mind chatter to dominate our thoughts or to quiet the mind and observe what we're thinking and feeling.

By quieting our mind, learning to listen to the small, still voice within and trusting the guidance we receive, we are guided back to our true selves. We're reconnected to that part of us that leads us towards love, towards living a life filled with purpose, joy and fulfillment. It's the part of us that trusts in ourselves and in our ability to make the best decisions for our lives.

Is this an easy journey? No. It takes practice, commitment and the relinquishing of the lies we've been told all our lives. Most of us have been told (sometimes unintentionally) that we're not good enough, smart enough or worthy enough to have the life we desire. Who hasn't had a teacher, a parent, a sibling, a friend or authority figure shame you, guilt you, reprimand you for being you? We're made to feel ashamed if we're different or if we don't fit in; we feel that there must be something wrong with us. And it's so deep within our subconscious mind and the collective consciousness, we don't even realize the power it has over us.

That is, until now. In this moment you can choose which path you want to take. In the following chapters you can learn to practice releasing fear, the mind chatter of your mind, and embrace a new way of thinking and connecting with your true self. Or you can continue doing what you've always done. The choice is up to you. It's my hope that you're ready to embark on a new journey one that will provide you with the tools to liberate your fear forever. Now that I've identified what F.E.A.R. is and its source, let's review seven faces of fear that sabotage us from living our best lives.

"FEAR STIFLES OUR THINKING AND ACTIONS. IT CREATES INDECISIVENESS THAT RESULTS IN STAGNATION. I HAVE KNOWN TALENTED PEOPLE WHO PROCRASTINATE INDEFINITELY RATHER THAN RISK FAILURE. LOST OPPORTUNITIES CAUSE EROSION OF CONFIDENCE, AND THE DOWNWARD SPIRAL BEGINS."

– CHARLES STANLEY

Chapter 2

THE SEVEN FACES OF F.E.A.R.

Fear presents itself in many ways (some obvious and some veiled) in an attempt to delude us into thinking we're protecting ourselves. Because the ego works to control our thinking through fear, we often don't recognize that our thoughts and actions are actually coming from fear instead of love. Any time we judge or attempt to control others, it comes from fear. Blame, shame and guilt are common fear-based emotions that we inflict on ourselves or others as our ego works to keep us from connecting to our true self. Some of the fear we experience is readily apparent, like when we have to do something that makes us nervous. Let's say you're speaking in public or confronting someone about something they did or said. Nervous fear causes our hearts to race, our palms to sweat, gives us butterflies in our stomachs—it can even make us feel sick. Sometimes that type of fear prompts us to act with courage when we haven't done so before. We're out of our comfort zone, and we feel better having taken that step forward.

However, nervousness isn't what I'm covering in this chapter. The seven faces of fear are ways in which our ego keeps us stuck from moving forward in our lives. It prevents us from connecting to our IGS (internal guidance system) which stems from our connection to our true self, our Divine Intelligence. We've all experienced these seven faces at one time or another. It's when one or more of these dominate our thinking that fear is controlling our minds and our lives. As you read through these descriptions, I encourage you to think about how these may factor into your life.

anxiety

The first face of fear I'm covering is anxiety or worry. We all experience it at one time or another and it's physiologically evident when we're in it. During episodes of anxiety we're driven by thoughts of the past or future causing our minds to go on a wild goose chase of "what if." We're resisting the present moment based on a past painful memory and focusing on a reality that hasn't yet occurred.

When we're in highly anxious states, we may feel completely out of control, experience panic attacks, increased blood pressure or contracted breathing. The thoughts racing through our minds can be troubling at best, horrifying at worst. This face of fear stems from our fear of the future. We feel out of control in navigating our lives. We're disconnected from our sense of self and lack trust in ourselves, others and our IGS. In fact we don't even know how to connect with our IGS when we're in this state.

The negative energy that we create within ourselves perpetuates a helpless state of victim-hood. When we're constantly anxious or worrying, we don't trust that we have the inner guidance to point us towards positive solutions or results. Our thinking becomes narrow and we often feel like we're backed into a corner.

Most of what we fear in our self-inflicted anxiety never occurs. And even when it does, many times we don't have control over the circumstances, so worrying keeps us powerless to find solutions. What we focus on grows stronger in our lives, so constant anxiety or worry becomes a self-fulfilling prophecy because we feed it.

For example, if you're worried about losing your job and that's your focus, you'll start to make mistakes at work because your mind is inattentive to the present moment. It becomes a cycle of self-defeating thoughts and behavior resulting in more anxiety and worry. Being in this state saps our energy and leaves us feeling out of control.

So how do we return to a state of calm when we're anxious or worried? Stop whatever you're doing and breathe. Three focused, deep breaths will help to slow your heart rate and center you back to the present. The past and future don't exist when we keep our minds focused on the present. By breathing and focusing on the present moment, we can see the situation more clearly.

Once you're calm, ask yourself: "What's the likelihood that what I'm anxious about will actually occur? What's the worst case scenario?" Typically it's something you can overcome or resolve. The best solutions come when we're calm, confident and connected. When we trust that we have the power to find the solutions to our challenges, we're open to signs and possibilities Otherwise, we make decisions based on fear, resulting in less-than-desirable outcomes that lead to more anxiety and worry. It becomes a downward spiral of negativity and victim mentality. Through consistent practice and mindfulness, we have the power to reduce the impact of this anxiety. In addition to the breathing exercise I mentioned earlier and questioning yourself on the validity of your anxiety, repeating a mantra can often be helpful. The act of voicing a positive statement can be very calming and centering.

A mantra to repeat when you're feeling anxious: "I'm willing to let go of the future for now and allow myself just to be in the present moment."

The second face of fear is anger. Anger stems from feeling hurt, from the ego's belief in unworthiness. When we're angry, we feel that someone has wronged us in some capacity. Sometimes our anger feels justified, such as when you've been ripped off or deceived. It sucks! However, getting angry doesn't resolve the situation. It's the ego's way of keeping you out of control and a victim. When we understand that we're inherently valuable and worthy no matter what, we can choose to react differently to situations that anger us. We can choose not to take it personally.

Often the anger we feel towards another is actually towards

ourselves. When a friend of mine and his wife divorced, his wife moved herself and their two daughters several states away and only gave him short notice about their relocation. My friend felt angry and hurt (as anyone would in that situation). However, he stayed angry for years, inflicting emotional pain on himself and his ex-wife. Some of the anger he directed towards her was actually anger he felt towards himself for not moving closer to his children. He was afraid that he wouldn't be able to find a job where they moved and would be unable to support them financially. His anger then turned to guilt that he wasn't being a good enough father. His underlying belief was that he was somehow flawed, and that's why she moved his children away from him. However, her decision wasn't even about him, it was in response to her beliefs about herself.

Whenever you feel angry, ask yourself, "What is it that really is angering me?" Once you've identified the cause of your anger, ask yourself how it makes you feel victimized. From there, you are open to identifying the source of pain. Is it a memory where you felt belittled or humiliated? We've all experienced those emotions.

Confronting your anger doesn't mean that you'll never feel anger or even have an experience where it feels justified. It's how we *choose to react* that either places us in control of ourselves or under the ego's domain.

Next time you feel angry, remove yourself from the situation if possible. Take a break; don't respond immediately. Otherwise, you may regret it later. Ask yourself the aforementioned questions and discover who or what is really angering you.

A mantra to repeat when you feel angry: "I allow myself to release this anger and be open to the love and compassion that lies within me."

DePReSSION

Depression is the ego's idea of a party—a pity party. I know this face of fear well. Most people who know me would be surprised to know that I've had years in which I struggled with depression. Typically I'm seen as the eternal optimist, smiling, happy and caring. We all wear our masks, right? The first two to three years after my divorce I was depressed and didn't even realize it. If I could do it over again, I would've joined a counseling or a support group for divorce straight away. I didn't, and that's just part of my journey. However I don't recommend going it alone.

Depression stems from a fear of the future and gives rise to a sense of powerlessness over our lives. Typically when we feel depressed, we're grieving the loss of something: a job, a marriage, the death of a friend or relative. It starts with grief and then manifests into depression because we fear the "unknowing" of what's next and feel like we don't have any control over it.

We fear that the void we feel will never be filled again. We tell ourselves things like: "Where am I going to get a job? I'll never find one that pays as well."

Depression is also a form of self-hatred. When we're depressed, we feel shame, guilt and unworthiness. I remember feeling like such a failure after my marriage that I didn't believe I mattered. I felt worthless even though some part of me knew otherwise. When we're depressed, we view ourselves as completely separate from others and our Divine Intelligence. We feel hopeless, helpless, powerless and angry.

Depression often manifests in self-destructive behaviors like self-medicating with drugs, alcohol, sex, shopping, eating or gambling. The common thread to all of these behaviors is looking for a fix to fill the void within. Temporarily we feel good, yet because we feel powerless over our lives, the grief, guilt and shame surface again.

Certainly grieving is a natural human emotion. When we experience loss on any level, it's okay to feel sad, to grieve; in fact it's healthy. Through grieving we can acknowledge the loss we feel, honor it and then re-connect to our true Self and begin healing.

The key is in re-connecting, not staying in the pity party. When we allow ourselves to feel the sadness and then re-connect to our inner happiness, we move through the loss with greater ease.

Gratitude is a great way to shift from feelings of depression. If you're struggling with finding anything for which to be grateful, then find something that makes you laugh. A comedy, a friend, music or a book can all facilitate in lifting your mood. It's impossible to feel depressed or angry when laughing or feeling happy. From there you can feel gratitude and a greater sense of peace knowing that you have the power to change how you feel. Keeping a gratitude journal can help to put your life into perspective.

A mantra to repeat when feeling depressed:
"I am willing to allow myself to feel happy. I know that this, too, shall pass."

Procrastination

Let's face it. Most of us procrastinate at one time or another, particularly when doing things we don't enjoy. For me, that would be cleaning. I like having a clean home, yet scrubbing, mopping and dusting aren't my idea of a good time.

Procrastination is one of the ways our ego creates the fear of failure or fear of success in us. When we procrastinate, we put off an action that ultimately benefits us. I don't really like to clean, yet when I'm finished I feel a sense of happiness and accomplishment for how nice my home looks. It's the egos attempt to convince us that what we desire really isn't important, that we don't deserve it. It whispers to us: "You can do that later." "That's really not important." "Why would you want to waste your time doing that?" How about, "I'm just too tired to exercise, clean, study, write or work now." You might actually be too tired, yet when you consistently put off your priorities, you're not honoring or valuing yourself.

If you have a goal to run a 5k, for example, and you consistently make excuses why you can't go for a run, you're not going to achieve your goal. Then what happens? You feel guilty and start talking yourself out of it with self-talk like, "That wasn't that important to me anyway."

The ego is sinister in its attempt to keep us chained to its side. To stop procrastinating, start prioritizing what's important to you. Write it down and do it! Even if it's one thing a day, you'll feel good that you accomplished a step towards your desired outcome. Then congratulate yourself. So often we don't give ourselves credit when we're moving forward and taking action towards our goals. Hmmm, think I'll go clean my toilets now!

A mantra to repeat when you're procrastinating:
"I value myself enough to take action towards my goal right now."

CONFUSION

Sometimes when we feel confused we're not experiencing the feelings we typically consider as fear-based emotions. Confusion is one of the ways the ego attempts to derail us. When we're uncertain or unsure as to what we want or what to do next, we're stuck. We don't know how to move forward. We may feel that our life is missing something, that we're incomplete. It leaves us feeling unsettled, unsure and anxious.

Confusion is another way the ego distracts us from being connected with our IGS. We all experience confusion from time to time. In many situations it's a simple fix, like, "I'm confused; do I want a salad or a burger for dinner?" Not a big deal, right? Where confusion really holds us back as fear is when we feel uncertain about areas of our lives. For example, "I don't really like my job. I feel burned out, yet I don't know what other kind of work I'd like to do."

That lingering state of confusion leads us down the path to disillusionment, frustration and a general feeling of being unfulfilled. Because we're not connected to our IGS, we look outside ourselves to find clarity. However, all the answers and clarity we need lie within us. Sometimes we are guided to an outside resource that helps us to connect to our IGS, but ultimately we find the answers within. For example, I'm certified as a Passion Test facilitator. The process of the Passion Test helps you to get clear about your top five priorities. It's not the Passion Test that gives you the clarity, it's the process of taking it and connecting to your IGS that brings the clarity to the surface so that it sits at the top of your awareness.

When we're confused, we're resisting the flow of moving forward. We're resisting the inner calling of our soul. And whenever we're in resistance, we're in fear. When we're connected to our IGS, we allow ourselves to get quiet and listen to our inner voice and heart that guides us to know what is right for us. From there we can gain clarity as to our priorities, our heart's desires and where we want to place our focus.

Once we have clarity, it doesn't matter if what we desire seems impossible. The clarity and the focus towards that desire opens us to allow the steps and opportunities to show up. When we're confused, we don't even trust to take a step because we don't know what we want or where we're headed.

A mantra to repeat when you're feeling confused:
"I allow myself to connect with the still, small voice within knowing the clarity I seek is within me and it comes to me with ease."

overwhelm

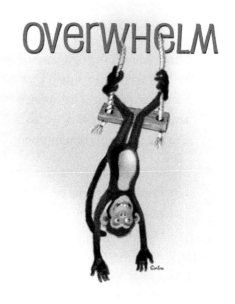

In our society feeling overwhelmed is a common experience. We're all busy. Our lives are filled with what we perceive as so much to do and not enough time to do it. It's easy to fall into this trap. As a single mom and business owner, I relate to this one oh so well. Overwhelm comes from a belief in lack or not having enough. Typically we're thinking, "There's not enough time. I have so much to do I can't do all of this myself. It's too much! Where am I going to get all the money to get all this work done? I'm so exhausted I can't take on one more thing." Am I hearing a collective "Oh yeah, I can relate to this?" You're not alone. We all experience it. It's another way that the ego keeps us disconnected, unfocused and in resistance.

Think about the last time you felt overwhelmed. Did you feel a sense of peace or calm? I'll wager you didn't. Overwhelm makes our minds run, constantly projecting what we need to do, how we're going to do it and by when. In other words, we're focused on the future and we're not in the present moment.

To quell the power of overwhelm we must come back to the present moment, take a breath and focus on the task at hand. Release everything else except what you're focusing on right now. By focusing on that one thing, whether it's for two minutes or two hours, you'll feel more connected to what you're doing, more relaxed and calm. The sense of overwhelm dissipates, and we become more productive. Taking things one step at a time, one task at a time with focus, puts your mind and body at ease and puts you back in control of your thoughts.

> **A mantra for when you feel overwhelmed:** *"All I have right now is the present moment. I allow myself to focus on that alone."*

rejECTION

When we experience rejection, typically we feel a sense of not being good enough. We don't get the job we want, someone ends a relationship with us, a friend gets angry with us or we go through divorce, and it's painful. We feel there must be something wrong with us, that somehow we're flawed.

But how about when we reject *ourselves?* For example, when we don't go for "our dream job" because we tell ourselves there's no chance we could get it anyway. Maybe we're dating someone really great that we like a lot, yet somehow we don't "feel it" for them. Are we rejecting love because we don't feel we deserve it?

I can think of two relationships years ago that I had with wonderful men that I ended because I wasn't "feeling it" or I had met someone with whom I felt a stronger "connection." In hindsight, I realized I ran from both of those relationships because I didn't feel worthy of the love and respect they felt for me. I kept going down the path of what I knew and where I felt comfortable, which ultimately led to pain again and again. Self-sabotaging behavior is another way the ego keeps us from love.

Whether it's a relationship, career or any aspect of our lives, rejection can knock us to our knees. If we allow it to send us into the "I'm not worthy or good enough" tailspin, we'll continually choose to go down the path to pain unwittingly. The ego is so deceptive it will tell us otherwise, and it will keep us from opening our hearts to ourselves and others. Until we truly love ourselves and give ourselves the gift of self-acceptance, self-worth, forgiveness, non-judgment and respect, we will close our hearts every time.

How often do you revisit guilt and shame about yourself or something you did in the past? How often do you judge and compare yourself to others? These are symptoms of self-rejection. We reject ourselves or others because it's too scary to open our hearts. In order for us to accept ourselves and others, we must first practice being kind and loving towards ourselves.

One way to do that is not to take anything personally. When we come to the awareness that how another person treats us is not about us (it's about their journey), we can accept rejection as part of our learning process. We can use rejection as a tool to recognize a misguided thought or judgment we have about ourselves or another person, and it opens us to feel compassion instead of anger, hurt and pain. This is not to say when a relationship ends or we don't get the job we want, we shouldn't or won't initially feel hurt. Allow yourself to feel the pain, yet understand that the pain is coming from your ego. Use it as an opportunity to become more aware of where you may be sabotaging yourself into believing that you're not worthy or good enough.

In my experience, I've come to believe that everything that happens to me is a learning opportunity. During the most painful situations where I've felt rejected, this belief has allowed me to open to learning from the pain and finding a gift in it instead of becoming bitter about it. Over time, I've come to understand why things worked out for my best interest, and you can too!

The common theme in these seven faces of fear is a belief in lack, either about yourself, "I'm not good enough, valuable enough, loveable enough," etc. or in situations: "There's not enough time, money, love, well-being." It's a belief that we live in a limited world and Universe.

Judging from the information that the media feeds us, it looks that way. There's starvation, war, economic hardship, loss of jobs, increased rates of disease—yet all of these problems are driven by fear from our ego-based society. When we look at the Universe it's constantly expanding, growing and changing. Think about the stars and planets that have just been discovered. Go outside at night and look at the sky. Is it limited? No!

In order for us to liberate ourselves from our fear, we must become unlimited by expanding our awareness, changing, growing and allowing ourselves to become the best that we can be. Reverend Michael Beckwith says, "The pain will push you until the vision pulls you."

Are you ready to liberate yourself from the seven faces of fear? It's time! We're being called to return to our natural state, our true selves, to reconnect with the Divine Intelligence within us, our IGS. We're being called to embrace the love that we are.

This journey is not for the timid. Our egos will attempt to drive us back into pain. We'll always experience pain and challenges that feel overwhelming, but when we focus on connecting with who we really are, we become stronger, brighter, more vibrant and resilient. That allows us to see the beauty of ourselves and others, to live from a place of love, joy and peace.

A mantra for when you feel rejected: *"I'm not my feelings, they represent old beliefs I'm ready to release. This too shall pass."*

"AS WE LOVE, WE SHALL BE RELEASED FROM PAIN, AND AS WE DENY LOVE, WE SHALL REMAIN IN PAIN. EVERY MOMENT, WE'RE EITHER EXTENDING LOVE OR PROJECTING FEAR, AND EVERY THOUGHT TAKES US NEARER TO HEAVEN OR HELL."

– MARIANNE WILLIAMSON

WHaT'S L.O.V.e. GOT TO DO WITH IT?

What is love? We have so many meanings for love we tend to compartmentalize it. We try to package it in a way that makes sense to us: romantic love, platonic love, parental love and so forth. However, in the end there is only love or fear. We either choose to live from a place of love or from a place of fear. It's not complicated. We make it complicated by trying to separate ourselves from others.

In our lives we are constantly making decisions, and we have different emotions based on fear or love. As I mentioned earlier, when we are functioning from a place of fear, we make decisions based on lack. It really comes back to that victim mindset and the belief that, "I'm not worthy" or "I'm not valuable." As Wayne Dyer states, fear comes from the ego "." So when we're living from a fear-based mindset, we're disconnected from our source. We view ourselves as separate from God and from others. We forget that we're connected to everything in the Universe.

When we're coming from a place of love, we know we are inherently valuable, worthy and deserving of the good that we desire for our lives. There's an inner connection to our true self we feel and trust. Call it intuition, your higher self, God, Source, Spirit, whatever you want name it, our IGS connects us to something greater than ourselves. From that connectedness, we can choose to live from a place of love, of trust, of knowing we are divinely guided in every aspect of our lives.

Right now I want you to think of someone or something you love. Go ahead, close your eyes, and think of that person, place or thing. How does your heart feel? Does it feel like it's expanding, joyful and open?

Look into the heart of that person. What do you see or feel? Go deeper, look into their Light, their essence of who they are. What makes them shine? Can you see those qualities within yourself? Do you feel your essence, your Light within you? There's no separation from it; it's always there within us.

Does being with that person or experiencing that special place or activity make you feel good, happy? How would it feel if you were happy *most of the time?* Would it change your life, your perspective? When we choose to live from a place of connection, we can choose to be happy. How? By loving ourselves.

Loving Ourselves, Valuing Everything

This is one of my favorite acronyms, because when we commit to love, our lives are transformed into a life of joy and peace. This is not to say we won't face challenges, heartache, frustration or disappointment. We will. Yet when we live from a place of love, we face those challenges from the perspective of non-judgment towards ourselves; everything happens *for* us not *to* us. We look at the people and the experiences of our lives as a training ground for joy, growth and expansion. Even challenges can become a means for us to connect more deeply with ourselves and others. The first step to living from a place of love is to let go of judgment about our past and future. So often we hold onto misconceptions we have about ourselves, about who we're supposed to be, and onto feelings of guilt and shame around our mistakes. A mistake is merely a learning experience, yet how often do we view mistakes as complete failures—as evidence that we don't measure up?

We often hold onto the mistakes-as-failures belief for years, feeling guilty about an action we took. What if you remembered that in every circumstance you did the best you could in that moment even if the best you could do during that moment was a mess? Even if you were screaming, yelling, crying, shouting words you *knew* you'd later regret, if that was your best in that moment, why not let it go? Why hold onto it like a treasure when all it does is weigh you down?

Love sees our imperfections, our shadow side, and embraces it as part of our wholeness. Life is messy. Relationships, work, family, friends, health and finances can bring us great joy and sorrow. However, when we concentrate on living from a place of love, we experience greater peace and joy. It emanates from us into all areas of our lives and into the world.

What are the ways in which we begin to live from a place of love? Three keys to loving ourselves are **self-acceptance**, **self-worth** and **self-respect**. When we accept, value and respect ourselves, a greater sense of inner trust is developed. We begin to trust our decisions and choices. When we make mistakes, we start to look at them not as failures, but as learning opportunities. Self-acceptance means learning to let go of your inner critic knowing that everything that shows up in your life serves a purpose in every area of your life.

Kicking out your inner critic means embracing all of yourself, especially the parts you don't like. How often does your inner critic whisper: "I shouldn't have done that. I'm so stupid. I'm too fat. I should be more successful. Couldn't I just get it right?"

Do any of these statements resonate with you? We all experience this negative self-talk, but we can minimize it by accepting that we're created inherently whole, complete and perfect. I can hear you saying: "But Carolyn—nobody's perfect!"

Well, I'm here to tell you to get rid of that thought. In the Divine Mind of Spirit, we are beloved human beings on this playground called Earth. There's nothing we have to change about ourselves.

Where we get stuck is when we view ourselves as incomplete and project our insecurities and fears onto others. When we can accept ourselves as we are, pimples and all, we become more receptive to accepting others as *they* are. Remember, we're all connected!

SELF-ACCEPTANCE

All of us have the capability to love and to hate. **Self-acceptance** opens the door for us to love ourselves and others with non-judgment, compassion and empathy. When you begin to judge what you got wrong, tell yourself to stop! Take a breath. Remind yourself you're doing the best you can. Easier said than done? Absolutely, but give yourself the gift of practicing the process. When you find your inner critic telling you all the things you need to change or how you need to be better, open yourself to accepting who you are in this moment and whatever is going on around you. Kicking out your inner critic is difficult, but the more you practice the faster you can return to the knowledge that you are whole and complete just the way you are. That's the first key.

SELF-WORTH

The second key, **self-worth**, is closely related to self-acceptance. Lack of self-worth creates much fear and pain in our lives. We've all been told we're not good enough on some level. Whether it was from a teacher, parent, family member, clergy, coach, friend, you name it—somebody told us we were faulty in some way. And we believed them, especially as children. We grow up with that belief tucked into our subconscious mind driving us to make fear-based decisions. We spend years trying to prove our worth. Sometimes we become do-gooders, and our actions have a positive effect on the world. Yet within us there's a belief that we can't do enough good because we're not worthy.

Sometimes a lack of self-worth manifests as arrogance, the fear masquerading as confidence. Any way that a lack of self-worth manifests, there's a belief that, "I'm only worthy based on what I do, what I have and/or other people's opinions of me." Nothing could be further from the truth. If we base our worth on something outside of ourselves, we'll never feel complete and whole. Our entire life will be spent trying to prove our worth, constantly striving to be someone other than who we are. Along with self-acceptance, self-worth stems from the belief that we're created whole, complete and perfect. It comes from knowing we are inherently worthy no matter how someone treats us or what they say to us. Just by being here on Earth, we are valuable. Our value is not dependent upon what we do, what we own or have. Until we value ourselves at the very core of who we are, we cannot value others in a deep and meaningful way.

When we value ourselves, we make choices based on what's in our best interest, not on what will please others or out of obligation. We speak our truth with kindness and firmness when necessary. We can say no with love and without resentment. When we value ourselves, we take care of our mind, body and spirit and allow others to do the same. We respect when others make choices based on what's in their best interest even if we don't like the choice they're making.

We're constantly making choices. And when we make choices based on love we make decisions with the belief that we are inherently valuable and worthy and deserving of good. Our perspective shifts to a viewpoint where there is abundance for everyone including ourselves and where the highest and best good is always opening up for us. We remember our connection and feel it. I think I said this earlier; it's the attitude of everything always happens for me. So even during challenges everything's happening for you to help you along your journey, to help you with your own evolving, wisdom, and growth; and so we're living every day from this place of greater peace and joy. Our decisions then come from a belief that I am enough, there is enough, and everything always works out for me.

If you find it difficult to wrap your head around this, start by doing a gratitude journal for a minimum of a week, and write down every day 3-10 things for which you're thankful. It could be very basic, something as simple as being thankful for your hands, and that your hands are pain free. I'm thankful I have enough food to eat. My mother has pulmonary fibrosis, and she is on oxygen now all the time. Some days I think, "I am so thankful that I breathe easily." There are so many things we take for granted. When you begin thinking and living from a place of gratitude, thankfulness and looking for the good in your life, you're going to find more good, and more blessings will begin to appear.

The third key to love is **self-respect**. Respecting ourselves means honoring ourselves, our time, our health and our bodies. We care for ourselves by taking care of our mind, body and spirit. We also keep commitments that we make to ourselves, whether it's to get enough rest or eat healthy foods, to exercise, meditate, focus time and energy on our priorities, or play and have fun. But how often do we put others before us and have no time left for our own care?

Self-respect also means being able to say no. Perhaps it's a favor we're being asked, and we feel obligated to say "yes." It could be a work commitment that we know is not in our best interest or trying to please a family member or partner in a relationship. When we say "yes" and know it's not in our best interest, we're not respecting ourselves.

When we begin to respect ourselves it becomes easier for us to respect the decisions of others even when we don't agree with them. Expecting to be respected by others when you don't respect yourself is like expecting a ripple on the water before you've thrown in the pebble. Respect must come from within first before we can give it.

We've all come across people with big chips on their shoulders who demand respect from whomever they encounter, whether it's in a restaurant, grocery store or at the mall. They have a negative attitude and want lots of attention because inside there's not a lot of self-love. In fact they loathe themselves, yet they're seeking respect outside of themselves. As from within, so it is without. Everything we experience in life comes from what we believe about ourselves.

When we begin to live from a place of love, we appreciate ourselves and others more. We can let our guard down, see the good in everyone and let go of trying to control the outcome of situations in our lives. We begin to trust that everything works out for us even when we can't see light at the end of the tunnel. Having self-respect is another way we can begin to live in the present moment, trusting that we'll be guided to our next step.

It gives us permission to take a breath and enjoy life, to view each day as a new beginning. Wouldn't it be great if everyone lightened up a little bit?

We're all so damned serious (even me sometimes), so focused on what we have to get accomplished. Goals are important, yet how much joy do we lose because we allow ourselves to feel stressed by situations and people in our lives? When we begin to live from love instead of fear, we create connections and a safe space for people to truly be themselves when they're with us. We can let go of judging ourselves and other people. We can relax and appreciate the differences and unique perspective that others have.

When we view our life as a gift to be enjoyed and shared, it allows us to live from a place of gratitude and to take responsibility for our own lives and happiness. I love this quote by Eleanor Roosevelt:

> "In the long run, we shape our lives, and we shape ourselves. The process never ends until we die. And the choices we make are ultimately our own responsibility."

We're constantly given the opportunity to choose; to choose how we feel, how we treat ourselves and how we treat others. When we choose love, life takes on a greater sense of ease, adventure and fun. We learn to accept what's showing up in our lives. We learn that through all the peaks and valleys of life we're always being guided to something better. After all, we're in control of how we feel, and despite the surrounding chaos, we can still *choose* peace and happiness. Learn to live from a sense of fullness and gratitude, and when fear comes (and it will), you'll know how to bring yourself back to love. It takes practice, but each time you experience a fear-based feeling it will become easier to recognize it, move through it, have gratitude for what it's teaching you and let it go.

Are you ready to liberate your F.E.A.R.? In the following chapters I'll guide you through more ways to overcome your fear and connect with living from a place of L.O.V.E.

A mantra for self-love: *"I love, respect and accept myself just as I am."*

"LOVE TAKES OFF MASKS THAT WE FEAR
WE CANNOT LIVE WITHOUT AND KNOW
WE CANNOT LIVE WITHIN."

– JAMES A. BALDWIN

Chapter 4
THE PRESENT OF PRESENCE

One of the ways the ego keeps us in a state of fear is through our endless mind chatter. Monkey chatter, as some call it, is that negative self-talk recording that is always going on in our heads. It causes us to focus on the past or worry about the future. This is the source of the majority of our fear-based thinking and suffering. Monkey chatter comes in two forms. We either rehash over and over again past situations that were painful, made us angry, annoyed or frustrated, (and hold onto those emotions) or we envision what's going to happen in the future by worrying about it. We stress over it even though it hasn't yet taken place. Either way we're screwed.

How do we stop the monkey chatter that drives our fear? By learning and practicing to focus on the present moment. All spiritual philosophies teach us the power of the present moment. However, staying in the present can be difficult, given our society's directive to multi-task. Multi-tasking drains energy and productivity. Present moment focus, on the other hand, allows us to detach from fear by just staying in the now.

Monkey chatter is the ego's way of derailing you from focusing on the present. For example, let's say you have a bill coming due. Cash is tight, and you have no idea how you're going to pay that bill. When you allow the monkey chatter to dominant your thoughts, it may go something like this:

> "Oh no, my phone bill is due next week, and I barely have enough money to pay my credit card bills. How am I going to pay it? I never have enough money. There's no way I'm going to be able to pay that, and my phone's going to get cut off again. I'm so stupid. Why can't I get a better job? How am I ever going to be able to get out from under all my debt? I'm always going to be broke!"

This incessant chatter goes on and on until you're in a state of anxiety, worrying about a future which has yet to occur. The ego loves this because it has complete control of your mind, and it keeps you stuck in a place of fear. Author Eckhart Tolle describes this as the "anxiety gap." It's where our unconscious mind, a.k.a. the ego, takes over our thinking and our emotions. He states in

The Power of Now, "… if you are identified with your mind and have lost touch with the power and simplicity of the Now, the anxiety gap will be your constant companion."

Here's an exercise. Once the monkey chatter starts, recognize the downward spiral of your thoughts, take a deep breath and say, "I know where you're trying to take me my friend, and I'm not going down that path." The very act of recognizing monkey chatter for what it is helps bring your awareness back to the present. By consistently focusing on the present and pushing monkey chatter away when we start to hear it, we can come to a feeling of peace. The space between thoughts is where we find peace, which opens us up to the possibility of solutions.

Conscious meditation is one way of reaching that space. Meditation practitioners are taught to let go of their thoughts, to focus on their breath and just "be." For many this seems impossible because the key is not to try to stop the thoughts or to judge them when you find your mind wandering (because it will). It's letting those thoughts go, and coming back to the present moment.

This same practice works in our daily lives. Tom Sterner writes in *The Practicing Mind*, "When we are totally focused on the present moment and in the process of what we are doing, we are completely absorbed in the activity."

Focusing on the present, what we are doing, our surroundings, the smells, what we see and hear brings us back to the now. How often do you accomplish a routine activity without even being aware of what you're doing? Have you ever driven somewhere and when you got to your destination you couldn't remember driving there? Yeah, me too. Your subconscious goes on autopilot while you think about other things. However, you have the power to change your focus by being present to what you're doing.

For instance, the next time you eat a meal, instead of gobbling the food down while watching T.V., focus on what you're eating. Deliberately pay attention to what you taste. How does the food smell? What's the texture? What flavors are you tasting on your tongue and in your mouth? Practice chewing slowly staying present while you're eating your meal; you'll be surprised how much more you'll notice about your food choices.

Focusing on the here and now takes practice and patience. It also requires us to allow ourselves to feel what our fear is bringing up and to accept those feelings in the present. Too often we try to shut our feelings out by staying busy or thinking about something else. Shoving our feelings aside or ignoring them creates stress, which is mentally and physically exhausting and unhealthy. Experiencing feelings of fear is really a sign we're ready to release ego-driven false beliefs. Allowing yourself to recognize these feelings by staying present to them is a form of self-acceptance. It's a gift fear brings us. Instead of being overcome by it, we can choose to use our fear as a guide to show us what we're ready to release so we can return to our natural state of connection and love.

Recognizing and toning down the mind chatter and practicing to focus on the present moment can be challenging. In fact, it may seem like a lot of work! However, the benefits to staying present far outweigh the costs in effort and practice. The main thing to remember is to recognize your feelings of fear when they crop up and to practice ignoring the monkey chatter. Here are three tips to releasing the fear the ego causes when we forget to stay present.

> **Breathe**. Whenever you begin to feel a sense of anxiety, fear, anger or overwhelm, stop what you're doing and take three deep breaths in and out. Focus on your breath. Do more if you can, but three alone will help you feel more centered.

Become present to what you're doing. What actions are you taking? What tasks are you doing? Look at your surroundings; observe colors, smells and sounds. Pay attention to your actions, and focus on being fully present no matter what you're doing.

Reconnect to your inner sense of well-being. Complete steps 1 and 2 then take a moment to close your eyes and feel your oneness with the Earth and Source. Even if it's just for a minute, you can loosen ego's grip and let your Divine light in and return to your natural state of love and well-being.

By practicing staying in the present moment not only will we become the master of our fear and our lives, we'll become more peaceful and joyful because we've chosen to relinquish the ego's grip on our minds. We come home to a place of peace.

A mantra to help you focus on the present moment:
"The past and future do not control me, the only moment I have is now."

"EXPOSE YOURSELF TO YOUR DEEPEST FEAR;
AFTER THAT, FEAR HAS NO POWER, AND THE
FEAR OF FREEDOM SHRINKS AND VANISHES.
YOU ARE FREE!"

– JIM MORRISON

Chapter 5

Your THOUGHTS, OBSErver or Prisoner?

When you're experiencing a fear-based emotion like anxiety or anger, typically you're so steeped in the feeling it's like a demon that possesses every part of you. Your mind races with the possibility of what could happen or with a memory from what happened before. Your heart races, too, and your body reacts by contracting, whether you hold it in your gut, in your back or feel an ache in your heart. Like an excited monkey, your ego takes over and you feel as if you've lost control of your mind and feelings.

Insane? Perhaps. What was once nature's self-protection mechanism becomes your adversary, and it happens to all of us.

The scene can go like this. You think about a person or situation from the past and it brings up sadness, anger, resentment or jealousy. Then your mind starts to speculate:

> "What if I don't hear from them? When will I hear from them? Oh, what if I don't get this job? Oh, God, how will I support myself and my family? What if I go into more debt? How am I going to pay my mortgage? What if we lose the house? If they don't hire me where am I going to find a job? I just wish they'd call and let me know. God, my life sucks!"

Negative self-talk spins out of control and you're thinking of situations and scenarios that probably will never happen. You've made yourself miserable (sometimes even sick) by conjuring up these thoughts in your mind.

So when our thoughts and feelings are running amuck and we feel completely overtaken by fear, how do we bring ourselves back to a place of peace? How do we grab that excited monkey before its chatter possesses us and takes us down the road to hell? How do we return to love?

One way is to by becoming the observer of your fear. By this I mean just allowing—not shutting down those feelings—allowing yourself to feel them and to detach yourself by observing what you're resisting. Remember that any form of fear is the ego resisting our Divine connection to Source. In Thomas Sterner's book, *The Practicing Mind*, he recommends a practice he calls, "Do, Observe, Correct." It's a process to use when you're doing work or practicing, like when you're playing a sport or music. But I believe it applies to many areas of our lives including dealing with fear.

For example, let's say a situation arises and you begin to feel angry. At that moment, become aware and present to your anger. In other words, become conscious that you're feeling angry and begin to focus on the present moment. What is it about this situation that's causing you to feel such anger? Feel it, recognize it and then observe yourself in it. Begin to picture yourself as if you were observing your behavior. What would you see? With this awareness we can begin to detach from our emotions and recognize that we alone have power over how we feel. The observer allows us to return to a state of calm, of connection to ourselves by stepping back and detaching from our fear.

I love the practice of yoga. It helps me physically, emotionally and spiritually. When I'm in yoga class, I am focused on the present moment, of each asana or posture. During class I give myself permission to just be here, in the now, and to put aside any other thoughts or things on my "to do" list until after class. In yoga, there are three asanas called "The Warrior." One of my yoga instructors, Chris Sims, guides us through these asanas. During warrior one he says, "Look at what it is you're fighting." In warrior two he tells us "see into it," and in warrior three he guides us to "see through it."

So just like the "warrior" in yoga, first look at what you're resisting. Where's the source of the fear? Then look into it as the observer. How are you reacting? What toll is it taking on you emotionally and/or physically? And finally, look through it. All fear is a call for love. It's a call for us to remember our oneness with the Divine and all of life. It's a call for us to remember we're inherently whole, worthy and complete. You may be thinking, "Sure, easy for you to say. Jump into the chaos of my life and let's see how peaceful you feel." The beauty of beginning to understand our fear is that we can let go of the judgment we put on ourselves. Learning to liberate ourselves from our fear and embrace the love that we are, takes practice. We're not going to get it perfectly, and that's O.K.

Sometimes we're so taken over by our fear it's hard to become the observer. How can you allow yourself to shift when you feel so out of control? When you're able to step back and be the observer and be the supporter, and consciously choose what you want to do in a situation, it gives you a greater sense of power, and a greater sense of freedom. However, before you can get to that place of calm where you're making conscious choices, you have to do whatever you need to in the short term to shift. In my **Free Your Fear**™ **Process**, I have steps that can help you do that. The first step is asking yourself, "What's causing me to feel this way?" The next step is to step back and say, "Okay, if I was looking down on myself, if I was observing myself as a friend, a mentor or an angel, what would I tell myself?"

When you do this, the answer is often, "Why am I so worried about the situation?" or "Why do I feel so fearful about this?" or "Why am I allowing myself to feel so hurt, or angry when I have no control over other people's behavior?"

Remember that other people's behavior is not about you. Don't take anything personally. These steps give you the opportunity to step away from yourself and look more objectively at what you're feeling. Then you can correct your behavior by asking, "What can I do differently?" Being an observer opens you up to learning about what triggers you and how you want to react the next time those feelings begin to surface. It places you in control because ultimately you're the only one in control of your feelings.

Our Source or true self comes from love, not fear. "Do, observe, correct" is a process of practicing and creating new patterns of thinking that align us with that Source. As the observer if we're judging our behavior negatively, the ego still has control over us. So as the observer we want to look at ourselves with love as in the innocence of a young child, gently, unconditionally and with a sense of humor. We all make mistakes, we all sometimes say things we wish we hadn't or do things we later regret. Sometimes despite our best efforts we still go to the fear even when we know we're doing it. The important thing is to keep practicing and don't beat yourself up. As the observer, give yourself permission to treat yourself as your best friend. What would you say to your best friend if he or she were in this situation? How would you treat them? You may go up and hug them and say, "Hey you know — why are you so anxious about this or what is it about the situation that makes you feel so scared? It's going be O.K. I love you. I'm here for you." So often we'll do for others what we won't do for ourselves.

What I'm suggesting is that when you practice self-love (in a non-judgmental way), you can be both observer and supporter for yourself:

> "Okay, I feel really anxious, yet I know that I can love myself through this. I'm going to the love. I don't have to go to the fear because I am powerful. I'm in control of my emotions and behavior so I get to choose."

Even if you're stuck in the feeling of hurt, anger, anxiety or whatever form the pain takes, you can observe that's where you are right now and not judge it. Accept it and know it will change. That alone is powerful because it doesn't have to control you.

When we allow ourselves to become the observer of our fear, we learn to feel it without judgment. From there we disarm its power to control us and open ourselves to return to our natural state of peace and well-being.

A mantra for observing the excited monkey mind:
"I am the conscious observer of my thoughts and feelings".

"WITH EVERYTHING THAT HAS HAPPENED
TO YOU, YOU CAN EITHER FEEL SORRY FOR
YOURSELF OR TREAT WHAT HAS HAPPENED
AS A GIFT. EVERYTHING IS EITHER AN
OPPORTUNITY TO GROW OR AN OBSTACLE
TO KEEP YOU FROM GROWING.
YOU GET TO CHOOSE"

– WAYNE W. DYER

Chapter 6
Obstacle or Opportunity

In the last two chapters I've provided ways to help you disarm fear's power over your thoughts and feelings. When we're able to remove the ego's domination over our thinking, we can begin to look at our fear as a teacher. How many times have you looked back at a painful or difficult period of your life and said, "Wow, I really learned a lot from that. I became stronger and wiser because of that experience?" For me those valuable lessons help me to awaken to my true nature, to gain clarity about the false beliefs I've held about myself and others. With each "lesson" I've become more self-confident and willing to let go of that which doesn't serve me. It helps me move forward in my life with anticipation and excitement instead of fear. That's the key to allowing fear become your teacher instead of your adversary.

Whenever you're thinking or acting from a place of fear, you have a choice. You can believe the circumstance is an obstacle or believe it provides an opportunity for you. You can choose to stay in fear, to be angry, resentful and stubborn in your belief that you're right, that you're the victim, or you can choose to reconnect with your true self and ask, "What opportunity is here for me now?" "What can I learn from this?" "What am I ready to let go of?"

Let me share an example. I learned many lessons about myself through this experience. Since my divorce, there's a man with whom I became friends. As I got to know him, I began to love him—really love him as a friend and potential partner. I saw and felt the possibility of a great relationship between us, yet for months the friendship remained platonic. After about six months of hanging out together we both admitted our attraction for one another and began to date. He was honest about feeling confused and uncertain about his feelings, and yet I thought he was willing to go on this journey with me, to explore the possibility that I saw and felt. Everything seemed so right!

We were compatible, had stimulating conversations, talked and laughed and openly communicated with each other. And the attraction we felt sizzled with passion. Yet within a short time, he told me that as much as he cared for me, as much as he liked me, as much as he was attracted to me, he didn't feel the connection he thought he should feel in a romantic relationship.

I felt hurt, disappointed and sad that this man I loved so much didn't feel the same. I had a difficult time conceiving how it could be so good between us, yet it just wasn't there for him. We agreed that our friendship was important to both of us so we decided to remain friends. Despite feeling hurt I realized that what he was feeling wasn't about me, that it was something within him, and so I was willing to accept it and move forward as best I could.

About two weeks later we were having dinner together, and he asked me if I thought we really could just be friends. "Of course," I said, and he told me he had just met a woman he felt a connection with he hadn't felt in years. In that moment I felt like my heart had been ripped open. How could it be that he just meets someone and feels that kind of connection? I wanted to scream; my ego took hold of my emotions. That night I laid awake barely sleeping, crying and thinking about how I continued to sabotage myself in relationships. I felt so hurt, angry and frustrated that once again I was experiencing this kind of pain. I knew the waves of deep pain and anguish I felt were not because of him or this situation. It was the memory of past relationships where I'd felt so rejected and hurt coming to the surface.

All the insecurities, feelings of being unlovable, came pouring in. My heart felt torn open, my solar plexus contracted with a deep sense of loss. And it felt so unfair. I felt raw and angry that once again I was not the chosen one.

What was the trigger that sent me spiraling into a vortex of pain and suffering? It was the belief that there must be something wrong with me, that I was unworthy of having the relationship I desired, that I somehow was flawed. In spite of years of working to improve my self-esteem I was flooded with these emotions. Have you ever been there? I bet you have because we all experience it one time or another in our lives.

I knew my thoughts were ego driven, and yet the feelings that had surfaced were wreaking havoc on my sense of self. They were ego-dominated, and I knew I had edged God out. Even though I knew the source of my emotions, I still felt a great sense of loss.

Then it hit me that all the pain came from holding onto former beliefs about my worthiness. I wasn't staying in the present, I was making his choice about "me." In that moment I realized two things:

> His thoughts and feelings were a projection of his beliefs and perceptions, not an indication of my worthiness. I needed to get back to the present because I'd begun projecting thoughts and ideas about the future which I had no proof or evidence to support.

A few days later I was taking a walk one morning and focusing on being present. I still felt a sense of loss, and yet I knew that I was causing my own suffering. I came across a doe and fawn eating grass on a hill next to the path where I was walking. We startled each other. I slowed my pace and stopped, and the fawn moved closer to its mother. For a couple of minutes we just stared at each other, waiting to see what our next move would be. I enjoyed their beauty and being so close to them. I was completely in the present just enjoying the moment, and in that moment, I felt no hurt, no sense of loss.

I decided to continue on my walk and slowly walked away from them as they continued munching on the grass. It was then I realized when I allow myself to be in the present moment, I'm not allowing the fear of past situations or future events to control my current thoughts and feelings. At the end of my walk I had an epiphany. It became clear to me that I had to experience what I did with this relationship in order to let go of my beliefs of unworthiness that I continued to hold in my body and mind. I had to free myself from the ego's domination of my sense of self-worth.

I also realized how my ego kept me attracted to the same type of man because the ego wants us to stray from love. When we're in pain, we can't be connected to love. So we are attracted to what is familiar to us even if it's painful. Think about the areas of your life where the same situation keeps occurring whether it's in relationships, work, finances or health. It's because the ego keeps pulling us back to the pain because that's what we know. Until we make a conscious choice to change the patterns of pain, the ego will dominate our thoughts and behaviors.

By opening myself to look for the opportunity from this painful situation, I was able to shift long-held beliefs about myself and release them. From that space I began to feel gratitude for this man as my teacher and friend, and for the gift of learning this situation provided for me. I finally embraced that no matter what happens in my life or relationships, no matter how people treat me, it's a reflection of how they feel about themselves. How I choose to react is up to me. I'm the only one responsible for my happiness.

We attract people and situations into our lives based on how we feel about ourselves. What we see in others mirrors what we see in ourselves. There's a saying, "When the student is ready, the teacher appears." The challenges we face occur because we're ready to learn the lesson and move forward. When we continue to experience the same challenges over and over again, we haven't learned the lesson. We're given the opportunity until we choose to learn and let go.

How often do we allow ourselves to be victims because of the challenges in our lives? "He did this to me." "She said that to me."

"Why are you doing this to me?" Thoughts like these keep us victim to our ego and powerless over our emotions. They strip us from our natural state of peace and well-being. We view ourselves as separate from others and victims of our circumstances. Nothing could be further from the truth. Our connection to one another is universal. We're more alike than different, so when we view our challenges from a place of love, as well as compassion for ourselves and others, those obstacles become opportunities for healing and growth.

Obstacle or opportunity? Fear provides us with the opportunity to face what we fear and to learn from it. When we're feeling fear, we're turning away from what we want. We're pinching ourselves off from our true nature, which is love. When we recognize our fear for the illusion it is, we can view every challenge as a blessing knowing there's a gift in every situation.

Sometimes the gift isn't obvious or forthright in our awareness. It's said that hindsight is 20/20, and I've found that it may take years for me to see the gift in a given situation. Yet by viewing my fear as a teacher, facing it and opening to the greater awareness that comes through it, I've learned that it's through the fire that I find faith. It's through its lessons that I let go of my ego and return to my true self. That's where our power lies. When we're connected to our true self, we become the visionary for our lives.

We're no longer victim to our circumstances; we know we have the power over our thoughts and feelings, and no one else is responsible for our happiness and peace of mind.

A mantra for when you're experiencing a challenge:
"There's an opportunity for me in this situation. I choose to see it through the eyes of love. I choose peace."

"FORGIVENESS ENDS ALL SUFFERING AND LOSS."

– GERALD G. JAMPLOSKY

Chapter 7
LIBERATE YOUR FEAR

By now I hope you've come to understand that fear is driven by our egos as a way to keep us separate from our natural state of connection to the Divine within us and others. It lures us into believing that we're separate and that to survive we must suffer. It takes us into a nightmare scenario where our happiness can only be found outside of ourselves, that we can only matter or be valuable based on how we look, what we own, how much we earn, what we do and every other mandate we or society places on us.

We're constantly bombarded by these fear-based messages, and it gnaws at us even when we walk the road of love. The good news is that we have the power to free our fear. Through the practice of self-awareness and some of the tools I've provided in this book, you can transform the feelings of fear that arise from daily life to greater joy and happiness. The truth is that our natural state is one of acceptance, well-being, peace, joy, confidence and abundance… in other words, *love*.

What can we do to free our fear quickly when it arises? How do we begin to live from a place of connection when we constantly sense low-level stress in our lives? How do we liberate ourselves from the ego's grip on our thinking when we find ourselves going down the road to hell? In addition to the solutions I mentioned earlier in this book, there are other key practices you can implement to begin re-connecting with your true self, your Divine self.

Two Tools I Highly Recommend

> **Meditation:** There are many ways you can meditate. You don't have to sit on a meditation pillow and say "Om" for 20 minutes (although I'd recommend it). You can do a walking meditation, a guided meditation or light a candle and focus on its flame.

The point of meditation is the complete focus on the present moment, being fully in the now, connecting to the still, small voice within. Meditation brings many benefits, both physically and psychologically. It teaches us how to bring and keep our awareness into the present moment and the benefits of deep breathing clearing and cleansing our lungs. Researchers at Harvard are now studying how meditation and yoga benefit those with high levels of stress. They have found that meditation can actually change how genes are expressed![1]

Yoga: Yoga is another practice that's helped me tremendously. Like meditation, in yoga we focus on the present as we move through the asanas or postures. The breath, the body and the mind become one in motion, building focus, strength and serenity. There's no competition in yoga. You're there to practice each asana in the moment to the best of your ability at that moment. We learn to let go of judgment about ourselves, our bodies and our practice and just "be." Yoga provides physical benefits of improved balance, strength and flexibility. The combination of our breathing and asanas cleanse and detoxify our cells.

If neither one of these appeal to you, then try just getting out in nature and taking a walk. The act of walking in a natural setting relaxes the mind and stimulates the body, allowing your brain to "reset." Even if it's just a quick trip around the block, the exercise of walking allows you to de-stress and recharge.

Perhaps you have an exercise regimen you practice routinely. A good way to enhance it and to create a greater sense of connection is to be completely in the present as you exercise. Pay close attention to your body, not on what you did yesterday, the co-worker who pissed you off or what you have to do today. Don't let the ego get your mind in its vices!

It's important to remember that in order to experience an awakened consciousness, to return to the love that you are, you must liberate the vice grip of the ego and return to present moment awareness. With practice and focus, when you use these tools, you will begin to experience a shift in consciousness and a greater sense of joy and well-being.

I did it, and so can you!

What happens when we get struck by a spiritual two-by-four? We get a phone call with bad news? A friend or family member rages on us or disappoints us? A relationship ends or we lose our job? Challenges will show up in life—they happen to all of us from time to time, and by now you know that how we respond is *your choice.*

I explained earlier that during the first few years following my divorce I felt I couldn't get ahead. It seemed no matter what I tried, I failed.

However, during this time I also realized I needed a tool to liberate myself from fear-based thinking and to help me quickly return to a state of well-being and peace. I recognized that happiness came from within and that in order for my life to change, I had to change my thoughts, beliefs and feelings about myself and my life. It was during those challenging times that I created the **Free Your Fear™ Process.**

Initially I used these seven steps to help me shift from feeling depressed or anxious to a greater sense of calm and control. It helped me release the fear-based thinking that kept me as a victim to my ego and to reconnect with my true self and know that solutions were available for every problem or challenge I faced. I continue to use this process for myself whenever I'm experiencing fear in its many disguises. After using it multiple times, I began to share it with friends and some clients. Everyone found it to be helpful in changing their perspective and providing a greater sense of peace and empowerment.

In this book, I've shared some of the concepts and tools I use in this process to help liberate you from the ego's desire to keep you living in a state of fear-based thinking and to help move you into a consciousness based on love. My hope and intention is that through this knowledge you'll begin to live with a greater sense of empowerment, connection, joy and peace. If you'd like to learn more about the **Free Your Fear™ Process**, contact me at support@carolynbsullivan.com.

Finally, remember that the power to freedom lies within you. You can choose to liberate your fear and let love in, or you can allow the ego to continue to dominate your thoughts and life. It's completely your choice. As Marianne Williamson states in *A Return to Love*, "Our deepest fear is not that we are inadequate. Our deepest fear is that we are powerful beyond measure. It is our Light, not our Darkness, that most frightens us... ..."

Hopefully the lessons in this book have helped you Get the F(EAR) Out! Remember, you have the power to recognize fear as the ego's way of keeping you stuck. Learn from it, use it and conquer its hold over you, and you'll no longer be afraid. Open your heart and allow your light to shine, for it's *your* brilliance and light that the world is seeking.

 Namaste.

"I'VE LEARNED THAT FEAR LIMITS YOU AND YOUR VISION. IT SERVES AS BLINDERS TO WHAT MAY BE JUST A FEW STEPS DOWN THE ROAD FOR YOU. THE JOURNEY IS VALUABLE, BUT BELIEVING IN YOUR TALENTS, YOUR ABILITIES, AND YOUR SELF-WORTH CAN EMPOWER YOU TO WALK DOWN AN EVEN BRIGHTER PATH. TRANSFORMING FEAR INTO FREEDOM - HOW GREAT IS THAT?"

– SOLEDAD O'BRIEN

About The Author

 Carolyn Bennett-Sullivan has been a student of psychology, human behavior and spirituality for over 30 years. Through formal and practical experience she discovered the magic that occurs when living authentically and aligned with your hearts wisdom and guidance.

Despite 25 years of successful sales experience she longed to do more meaningful work. Through her divorce in 2010 and disappointing attempts to re-enter the corporate world of sales, life's challenges led her on a journey of awakening and self realization. It was through this process she discovered how to un-cage the chatter, reclaim control over her thoughts and re-connect to her internal guidance system creating greater confidence, clarity and happiness within herself. She loves connecting people with solutions to help them create a happier, more fulfilling life through her book, workbook, speaking and workshops.

She is the mother of a beautiful and bright daughter who provides her with laughter, love and learning on a daily basis. She currently resides in Wilmington, DE.

[1] Relaxation Response Induces Temporal Transcriptome

Changes in Energy Metabolism, Insulin Secretion

and Inflammatory Pathways

WOrk WITH Carolyn

Carolyn Bennett-Sullivan loves connecting people to solutions to improve their life. She provides the following *Get the "F" Out* products and services for more in depth awareness and expansion in your personal journey.

- *Get the "F" Out Workbook*

- *Keynote Speaker*

- *The 7 Faces of Fear Workshop*

- *What's Love Got to Do with It Workshop*

- *Free Your Fear™ Process Workshop*

Carolyn Bennett-Sullivan

Awaken your heart. Ignite your passion. Own your power.

To find more information about Carolyn visit her website
www.carolynbsullivan.com

resources

My journey of awakening and personal growth would not have occurred without the influence of Visionaries and teachers who've come before me. Listed below are resources that have helped me. This list certainly isn't comprehensive. This is merely a sampling of some of the offerings of those listed below. There are many paths and teachers to help you on your way to a better life; my hope is that along with my book and workbook you will find teachers who make a positive difference in your life.

Janet & Chris Atwood

The Passion Test

Your Hidden Riches
www.thepassiontest.com

Thomas M. Sterner

The Practicing Mind
www.thepracticingmind.com

Eckart Tolle

The Power of Now
www.thepowerofnow.com

Dr. Wayne W. Dyer

The Power of Intention

Excuses Begone

The Shift

I Can See Clearly Now

Wishes Fulfilled
www.drwaynedyer.com

Mark Nepo

The Book of Awakening

www.marknepo.com

Byron Katie

The Work of Byron Katie

Loving What Is
www.byronkatie.com

Aileen McCabe-Maucher and Hugo Maucher

The Inner Peace Diet
www.theinnerpeacediet.com

Colin Tipping

Radical Forgiveness

Radical Self Forgiveness

www.colintipping.com

Don Miguel Ruiz

The Four Agreements

The Mastery of Love

Warrior Goddess Training

www.miguelruiz.com

Ernest Holmes

The Science of Mind

Marianne Williamson

A Return to Love

Illuminata

Healing the Soul of America

The Age of Miracles

A Year of Miracles

www.marianne.com

Gerald Jampolsky

Love is Letting Go of Fear

Goodbye to Guilt

The "Oh Shit" Factor

www.jerryjampolsky.com

Jaden Sterling

The Alchemy of True Success

www.truesuccessbook.com

"THROUGH ALL THINGS LOVE IS POSSIBLE AND ALL THINGS ARE POSSIBLE THROUGH LOVE."

– CAROLYN BENNETT-SULLIVAN

CPSIA information can be obtained at www.ICGtesting.com
Printed in the USA
BVOW11s0008270116

434369BV00002B/2/P

9 780986 133107